DOING SMALL BETTER

a practical guide for faith-based leaders of small organizations

ISBN: 979-8-218-90117-2 (Paperback)

Published by:
Doing Small Better Publishing
Atlanta, Georgia, USA

First Edition

The views and opinions expressed in this book are those of the author and do not necessarily reflect those of any organization or institution.

Printed in the United States of America

Table of Contents

About the Author

Layne A. Fields is a faith-driven leader, pastor, and licensed residential contractor, whose life and work embody the message of *Doing Small Better*. With more than three decades of experience spanning business, ministry, and leadership, Layne has dedicated his life to helping small organizations, entrepreneurs, and faith-based leaders build with excellence, integrity, and purpose.

Born and raised in Riverhead, New York, Layne was a multi-sport athlete and team captain before earning a full basketball scholarship to Pace University, where he graduated with a Bachelor of Arts in Mass Media and a minor in Marketing. His collegiate years taught him the power of preparation, discipline, and teamwork — lessons that would later become the foundation of his leadership philosophy.

Over the course of his career, Layne excelled in corporate sales, entrepreneurship, and ministry environments — from top-ranked pharmaceutical and national account sales roles to pastoral leadership and small business ownership. He became a state-licensed residential contractor and home builder, earning credentials as a Certified Green Homebuilder, OSHA-certified professional, and U.S. Veterans Administration-certified contractor.

Beyond business, Layne's life is a testimony of resilience. After losing both his wife and mother to breast cancer within months of one another, he discovered that faith, perseverance, and purpose can be fulfilled while enduring life's painful experiences. A prostate cancer survivor himself, Layne's story became a living reminder that setbacks really can become steppingstones when you place your trust in God.

Today, through his consulting and speaking platform **Doing Small Better**, Layne inspires leaders to align purpose with profit and to approach business as both calling and stewardship. His message is simple yet powerful: *true prosperity is found in doing small things with great faithfulness.*

Layne resides in the Atlanta, Georgia area, where he remains a faith leader committed to shaping people, strengthening principles, and expanding possibilities — anchored in the belief that everything significant begins small and grows through steady faithfulness.

About This Book

Doing Small Better: A Practical Guide for Faith-Based Leaders of Small Organizations

---

In a world that celebrates "bigger, more, louder," **Doing Small Better™** reminds faith-based leaders that *faithfulness* is greater than fame and that pursuit of one's *purpose* is the true yardstick by which success is measured.

This book is a pragmatic and practical guide for small-business owners and other faith-based marketplace leaders to stay grounded in faith while pursuing profits with excellence, integrity, and purpose in every decision. It speaks directly to pastors, entrepreneurs, nonprofit directors, and marketplace professionals who are called to lead ethically, serve compassionately, and build sustainably.

You'll discover that true prosperity isn't found in the size of your organization, but in the strength of your convictions — in the balance between *purpose, practice, and profit.*

Each chapter weaves together biblical truth, real-life leadership lessons, and practical strategies that show how to build thriving organizations without losing your soul. Through stories of faith, resilience, and excellence, you'll see that doing small better means doing it with heart — honoring God in the details and decisions that leadership demands.

The goal is simple: to help you align your calling with your conduct so that what you build in business reflects who you are in Christ. Because when purpose guides your practice, and your practice produces honest profit, the result is what this book calls *true prosperity* — peace in your spirit, integrity in your work, and rest in your results.

Doing Small Better™ is more than a book — it's a blueprint for faithful leadership in uncertain times, where the intersection of *purpose, practice, and profits* means true prosperity.

Introduction – Doing Small Better Begins with You

Every great movement begins with something small — a spark, a seed, a single step of faith. But in today's world, small often feels like failure. We've been conditioned to equate big with successful, loud with impactful, and fast with fruitful.

Consider Bethlehem

"But you, Bethlehem Ephrathah, Though you are little among the thousands of Judah, Yet out of you shall come forth to Me. The One to be Ruler in Israel…"

— Micah 5:2 NKJV

God does His best work in the small. Consider Bethlehem, the birthplace of Christ. Bethlehem was insignificant on the world's map, but deeply significant in the mind of God. Christ's birth there reveals a divine pattern woven throughout Scripture—God often chooses small places to birth big purposes.

Jesus was not born in Jerusalem, the religious center; nor Rome, the political center; nor Athens, the intellectual center. Instead, the Savior entered the world through a small village, in a stable, laid in a manger. Bethlehem becomes a living reminder that God is not impressed by size, status, or fame. He values humility over prestige and delights in elevating what people overlook.

Its symbolism echoes the heartbeat of *Doing Small Better™*: God often begins His greatest work through small beginnings, overlooked places, and humble starts. In choosing Bethlehem, God declared to every generation, "Never despise small beginnings—My greatest work often starts there."

When I started in business and ministry, I believed that growth alone was the goal — more clients, bigger buildings, larger congregations. But over the years I've learned that bigger isn't necessarily better — *better* is better. And doing better doesn't begin with what's around you. It begins with what's within you.

A Shift in Perspective

"He who is faithful in what is least is faithful also in much."

— Luke 16:10 NKJV

At its core, Doing Small Better is about redefining what success looks like for faith-based leaders, entrepreneurs, and small-business owners. It's a call to reject the world's obsession with expansion and instead embrace the Kingdom's call to faithfulness.

You see, God doesn't measure success by scale; He measures it by stewardship.

This isn't just for Sunday sermons — it's for board meetings, job sites, classrooms, and client calls. It reminds us that what we do with the little things determines whether God can trust us with more. When you lead with integrity in the small, you position yourself for God to bless you with bigger, greater, and more in His time.

The Calling to Build Better

As a contractor by trade and a minister by calling, I've seen the parallels between building houses and building organizations. If the foundation is weak, it doesn't matter how beautiful the structure looks — the moment pressure comes, it will crumble. That's why so many leaders feel worn down or burned out: they've been focused on expanding the structure without strengthening the foundation.

This book exists to change that.

It's for every faith-driven professional who knows that your work is more than a paycheck — it's a calling. It's for every leader who's tired of compromising values for visibility, ethics for efficiency, or peace for progress. It's for those who want to grow the right way, where purpose and profit work together in harmony.

From Principles to Practice

Throughout this book, you'll find practical frameworks and faith-based principles designed to help you lead with integrity and excellence no matter your title or team size.

You'll learn how to:
- Build organizations that reflect God's character.
- Lead teams with compassion, clarity, and conviction.
- Pursue profit without compromising purpose.
- Rest in the peace that comes from doing what's right — not just what's easy.

These lessons are drawn from more than three decades of experience across business, ministry, and leadership — years that have taught me that the process matters just as much as the product.

You'll see that success built on shortcuts doesn't last — but success built on stewardship always stands.

Your Role in the Mission

Doing Small Better isn't just a catchy phrase — it's a movement.

It's a way of leading that honors God, respects people, and values excellence in every detail.

You don't have to run a mega-organization to make a meaningful difference. If you're leading with integrity, serving with humility, and pursuing purpose before profit, you're already doing Kingdom work. This book will help you do it with greater clarity, conviction, peace, and JOY.

So whether you're a small-business owner, a nonprofit director, a ministry leader, or simply someone trying to make a difference where you are — this is for you.

"Do not despise these small beginnings, for the Lord rejoices to see the work begin."

— Zechariah 4:10 NKJV

What's Ahead

Each chapter will walk you through a layer of the Doing Small Better framework:

We'll explore the Super Seven ethical standards — respect, honesty, excellence, responsibility, compassion, fairness, and citizenship — and learn how they become the building blocks of lasting impact.

You'll also find reflective sections, personal stories, and action steps that bridge faith with functionality.

By the end, my prayer is that you'll have not just read a book, but embraced a mindset — a new way to work, lead, and live that invites God into every decision.

Because when you do small better, you position yourself for divine promotion.

"Well done, good and faithful servant; you have been faithful over a few things, I will make you ruler over many."

— Matthew 25:23 NKJV

That's the heartbeat of this message. That's the foundation of this movement. And that's where your journey begins.

Preface – Why I Wrote This Book

There's a saying that experience is a great teacher — but I've learned that *reflecting* on experience is what truly brings wisdom. Over the years, through business highs and lows, and personal victories and heartbreaks, I've discovered that what matters most isn't how much you achieve, but how faithfully you live out what you've been called to do.

This book was born from both pain and purpose.

I've stood in boardrooms where decisions were driven by greed instead of grace. I've sat in sanctuaries where faith was preached but not practiced. And I've lived through seasons when doing "the right thing" came with a real cost — financially, emotionally, even spiritually.

But through it all, one truth has remained: God honors those who build with integrity, humility, and excellence — no matter how small their platform seems.

There was a time when I had to rebuild not just businesses, but life itself. My wife was fighting for her life in Decatur, Georgia while my mother was fighting for hers in Ocala, Florida. I'd drive down I-75 with tears streaming down my face every mile, praying for both of them — hoping for strength I didn't have.

My mother passed away first. Nine months later, my wife went home to be with the Lord. Two weeks after burying her, I lost my job. I was unemployed with two toddlers, a broken heart, and a faith that needed healing. In addition, I was pastoring a small congregation that was also grieving the loss of their First Lady and was looking to me for strength.

Yet even then, God was faithful. Through grief, He gave me grace. Through loss, He taught me valuable lessons. And through hardship, He revealed my purpose — to help others build lives, ministries, and businesses that can withstand the storms.

So when I talk about Doing Small Better, I'm not just sharing generic leadership principles. I'm sharing lessons from the furnace. I'm talking about building when you're tired, leading when you feel unseen, and trusting that faithfulness in the small things always prepares you for greater.

Over the years, I've been blessed to wear many hats — husband, father, contractor, pastor, sales leader, consultant — but the thread that connects them all is stewardship. Everything I have, everything I've learned, and everything I've survived belongs to God. My only goal is to manage it well and teach others to do the same.

When I first started writing *Doing Small Better*, I didn't set out to write a leadership book or a devotional. I set out to write a life book. One born from years of building, breaking, and rebuilding again — in business, in ministry, in faith, and in life itself. The lessons in these pages weren't learned from textbooks or seminars. They were learned on job sites, in hospital rooms, in prayer closets, and during quiet seasons of suffering when survival itself meant having to trust God for strength I didn't have, wisdom I didn't know, and peace I couldn't explain.

This book is a collection of those lessons. They've been refined through fire, tested through faith, and proven through practice. It's for every leader who's ever wondered if the small things still matter in a world that only celebrates the big.

I wrote this book for the business owner who feels overwhelmed, the pastor who feels isolated, the dreamer who's doing all you can with what little you have. I know the struggle because I've been there.

And I can tell you this with confidence: small done right becomes great in God's hands.

If this book helps you see your work as worship, your effort as excellence, and your faith as your foundation — then it's done its job.

So, before you turn the page, take a deep breath.
You're not behind.
You're not forgotten.
You're not too small.

You're exactly where God wants to show you that small done better still changes the world.

And if this book helps you find peace, purpose, and prosperity in your own journey — then every tear, every test, and every testimony that led me here will have been worth it.

Your friend,

Layne

Chapter 1

Purpose Before Profit

"But seek first the kingdom of God and His righteousness, and all these things shall be added to you."

— Matthew 6:33 NKJV

The Misplaced Metric

We live in a culture obsessed with numbers — sales numbers, follower counts, square footage, attendance, and profit margins. But God's scoreboard looks very different.

In the Kingdom, success is never measured by how much you have, but by how well you steward what you've been given. It's not the number of clients, members, or employees that define your success; but rather, it's your knowledge of purpose and your corresponding commitment to that purpose that defines success.

When you have a clear sense of purpose, you can pursue your work relentlessly, stand before a holy God with confidence, and dwell among men with integrity. It becomes a form of reasonable service, which is an act of worship unto God (Romans 12:1). Simply stated, when purpose drives the work, the work becomes worship.

Too many leaders today chase growth at the expense of meaning, confusing activity with progress and success with visibility. But God is less impressed by metrics and more impressed by one's faithful pursuit of purpose and unwavering obedience to the calling and assignment He's place upon your life. He's moved by motives not metrics. When your purpose is anchored in Him, profit becomes a by-product, not the main point.

The Purpose Principle

Purpose is the reason you start. It's the "why" that so many motivational speakers mention in their talks.

The danger for many leaders is chasing profit without anchoring it to purpose. That pursuit eventually leads to exhaustion, emptiness, and ultimately, burnout. I've watched leaders flourish financially and yet fail morally. I've seen ministries grow numerically and yet shrink spiritually.

In my own life as a leader, I can attest to the fact that every time I got distracted from my purpose, I lost sight of the true, godly measures of success, and the results of my efforts were mediocre at best.

Profit is the reward that follows when you start for the right reasons and remain focused on the right objectives. Profit alone will pay bills — but the fulfilment of one's purpose will build a legacy that echoes in time and eternity.

When your purpose aligns with God's principles, prosperity becomes sustainable because it's built on something eternal. The profits that follow then become more than rewards for your cumulative efforts, they become blessings from the Most High that are meant to reinforce obedience and motivate you to continue pursuing purpose. In fact, when you see that purpose has a tangible payoff, it should drive you to pursue it more aggressively, passionately, and consistently.

Purpose Protects

A clear sense of purpose becomes a moral compass which helps faith-based leaders navigate a decision-making terrain that is filled with twists, turns, traps, and unforeseen temptations. It helps identify opportunities that look good but aren't necessarily of God. Additionally, staying faithful to one's purpose also helps to clarify the distinction between good ideas and God ideas.

I've discovered firsthand that not every one of my good ideas were inspired by God. As a relatively creative person, I've pursued many ideas that seemed good to me but ultimately didn't line up with God's ordained purpose for my life and thereby yielded marginal results, if any.

At best, *if* my creative ideas were indeed inspired by the Holy Spirit, then my disobedience was found in the execution of those ideas or perhaps my miscalculation of the proper time to execute those ideas. Only time will tell.

The easy response would be to simply categorize those moments as trial and error, charge them to the game, take my losses, and move on to something else. However, a deeper, more humble assessment reveals that I missed the mark. I fell short of His glory. I missed God. I moved in my direction, and not His. I acted without going deeper into prayer over the matter and pursued my ideas apart from his good and perfect will. Yet, because He's gracious, he allowed me to operate under a permissive will, which protected me from my greatest adversary. Me.

Apart from the protective custody of God, my losses could have been far more devastating than they were. In such cases, the response isn't a cavalier "oh, well, my bad". But rather, a deep sense of contrition met with pleas for forgiveness, and genuine repentance that afforded me the grace of another chance.

I've also been so attuned to my purpose on occasion, that I've turned down projects that could've been lucrative but didn't align with my values or calling. I knew that if I compromised, I'd regret every minute of it. For me, the peace of mind and obedience to God were far more valuable than any monetary compensation. And because God is faithful, every time I've walked away from fast money, I've walked into lasting peace. Every time I rejected compromise, stayed true to my purpose, and practiced integrity, I can see where God openly rewarded me with better opportunities, healthier contracts, and more fruitful professional relationships.

When allowed to do its job, purpose will protect you from greed. Purpose will guard you from burnout. Purpose will sustain you through seasons when profit seems delayed. Sometimes, God slows down your progress to strengthen your perspective and use that time to clarify your true purpose.

> *"Commit your works to the Lord, and your thoughts will be established."*

> — Proverbs 16:3 NKJV

When purpose is clear, temptation loses its power. You stop chasing opportunities and start stewarding assignments.

The Profit Myth

Let's settle this once and for all: profit is not evil. In fact, profit is biblical.

In the parable of the talents (Matthew 25:14-30), the servant who multiplied what he was given received the master's reward — not because he hoarded it, but because he increased it. The issue isn't profit itself; it's when we allow profit to supersede purpose that we run the risk of going down a path of disobedience.

Profit should never come at the expense of your people, your peace, or your principles.
When you chase profit over purpose, you'll end up rich in numbers and poor in joy. Rich in possessions and poor in character. Rich in influence, but poor in meaningful relationships. Perhaps this is why people who are successful in worldly terms are often unhappy, depressed, and unfulfilled by riches, fame, and all the deceptive accoutrements they accumulate along the way.

Profit is not evil. Purpose is not optional. But separated, they are dangerous. Profit without purpose leads to greed. Purpose without profit leads to burnout. Profit is the fuel that moves the vision forward. Purpose is the driver that ensures you're headed in the right direction. When purpose and profit unite, you discover true prosperity. The best businesses unite them — they serve people, build relationships, make a difference, and yes, they make money too.

Purpose keeps profit in its proper place — as a by-product of obedience, not the object of worship. When you build for God's glory instead of man's applause, profit will follow purpose naturally, without compromise.

Integrity- The Companion of Purpose

If you want to know what really holds a faith-based endeavor together, it isn't contracts, cash flow, or clever marketing — it's integrity.

"The integrity of the upright will guide them, but the perversity of the unfaithful will destroy them."

— Proverbs 11:3 NKJV

Integrity is the invisible companion of purpose that keeps you on course when profits, pressures, and people try to pull you in every direction. Without it, you're just drifting. With it, you'll always find your way forward.

Integrity isn't about perfection — it's about consistency. It's about doing the right thing even when no one is watching. It's about keeping your word when it costs you something. It's about building a name that others can trust.

I've seen contractors promise the world only to deliver mediocrity and broken trust. I've also seen businesses with less flash but more integrity thrive because their good name was worth more than any marketing campaign.

Integrity may not always pay immediately, but it always pays eventually. It guides your steps, guards your reputation, and gains the favor of God and man.

The Currency You Can't See

Integrity is like credit. You can't always see it, but it's always working behind the scenes. When people know you as a person of integrity, they'll lend you trust, opportunity, and grace. But once integrity is broken, it takes years to rebuild — and some doors may never open again.

Deals fall apart. Partnerships sour. Reputations collapse. And often the failure doesn't come right away; it comes later, after trust has been eroded piece by piece. Guard your name like treasure. Because in business and in life, integrity is the currency you can't afford to lose.

Integrity in Small Things

We often think about integrity only in terms of big moral decisions — don't lie, don't cheat, don't steal. But integrity shows up in the little things too.

- Do you keep your word when the contract isn't in writing?
- Do you pay suppliers and subs on time, before paying yourself?
- Do you admit mistakes instead of covering them up?

The world may call these "small things," but in the Kingdom of God, small things reveal the size of your heart. Small things expose the content of your character. Integrity in the small adds up over time to accumulate the credibility needed to scale sustainably.

Integrity is Liberating

When you practice integrity, you don't have to look over your shoulder. You don't have to wonder if the truth will catch up with you. You don't live with the anxiety of being exposed. Integrity is freedom. When you walk securely, you can lead confidently, love boldly, and sleep peacefully.

I remember a season early in my contracting career when a client asked me to overlook something on a job site that wasn't up to code. "No one will know," they said. "It'll save us both some money." On paper, it looked like an easy win. But I knew that once I said yes to compromise, I was selling more than my reputation — I was selling my peace.

I won't lie. I thought about it long and hard. But when the Holy Spirit arrested me and brought me back to my senses, it became clear that in the event of a mishap related to that compromise, all liability would fall on me. If someone got hurt, I'd be sued. If someone died, a guilty conscience would have eaten me alive.

Instead, I used that situation to operate like a licensed professional should by practicing integrity, and by maintaining my Hippocratic duty to the State of Georgia, which issued my license. And, ultimately, by honoring God with my actions.

I assured the client that I would do things the right way. I paused the job, applied for the proper permits with the city, and executed the scope of work properly. The work passed all inspections, and we lived to fight another day with a clear conscience.

That one decision, built credibility with my client, inspectors, subcontractors, and even future clients who heard how I conducted myself. Not compromising my integrity almost cost me a contract, but compromise could have cost me everything, and I vowed to never make that exchange.

Purpose Precedes Provision

I've learned that God never provides where He hasn't given purpose. When you commit to the assignment He's placed on your life, He sends what you need — people, resources, opportunities — at the right time.

The greatest mistake many leaders make is trying to fund something before they find their purpose. Purpose is what attracts provision. It's the magnetic force that pulls the right support into place. So, before you pray for profit, pray for clarity. Ask, "Lord, why did You trust me with this business, this ministry, this team?"

Once that answer is revealed, profit will find its rightful place — not as your master, but as your servant.

Practical Takeaways

1. Do Right Even When Wrong is More Profitable
2. Keep Your Word Even When it Costs.
3. Choose Peace of Mind Over Profit- You Won't Regret It.
4. Choose Long-Term Purpose over Short-Term Compromise
5. Clarify Your Purpose.
6. Check Your Motives.
7. Pray for Alignment.

Reflection & Action Steps

1. Write your organization's "why" in one sentence.
2. Ask yourself: Would I still do this if no one noticed?
3. Align your next three leadership decisions with your long-term purpose, not short-term applause.
4. Take time this week to pray over your goals and surrender your plans to God's purpose for your life.

Closing Thoughts...

Purpose and Integrity are the foundation of Doing Small Better. They're not glamorous. They aren't flashy. But they make the difference between a leader that crumbles and leadership that lasts.

Profit may buy success for a season, but purpose and integrity build a legacy for a lifetime.

Before you can build anything meaningful, you must first know why you're building. Purpose is what anchors you when profits fluctuate, when followers fade, and when momentum slows.

Purpose and integrity clarify priorities. They determine what deserves your yes and what requires your no.

True prosperity doesn't start with profit — it starts with purpose and continues with integrity. Because when purpose is clear, decisions become simple, integrity becomes instinctive, and work becomes worship.

Chapter 2

Stewardship: The Blueprint for Faith-based Leadership

"Moreover, it is required in stewards that one be found faithful."

— 1 Corinthians 4:2 NKJV

Leadership Begins With Stewardship

Faith-based leadership isn't about authority — it's about accountability. It's not about ownership — it's about stewardship. Every position we hold, every team we lead, and every vision we cast is a trust from God. We don't own them. They're entrusted to us.

Subsequently, the fruit born from prayerful, faithful, and careful stewardship of God's trust does not belong to us either. It all belongs to God. We don't own the outcomes. We simply manage the opportunities. This is where many leaders, including me, stumble and struggle by confusing stewardship with ownership and overlooking the seriousness of the call to manage God's people, and God's resources God's way.

God didn't call us to control outcomes — He called us to manage our obedience to His will. It is our righteous management of this trust that makes faith-based leadership fulfilling despite its many challenges. I understand this firsthand, because every time I lost sight of the call to stewardship, the ensuing struggles, lack of fruitfulness, and outright exhaustion were overwhelming. On the other hand, when I functioned within the guidelines of stewardship, God lifted the load and carried the burdens, thereby allowing me to experience the joy of leadership even when times were difficult.

"The earth is the Lord's, and all its fullness."

— Psalm 24:1 NKJV

Everything we build ultimately belongs to Him. When you understand that truth, your leadership posture changes. You stop striving to prove yourself and start serving to please Him. Faithful leadership begins when you stop chasing authority and start cultivating a culture of accountability to God from yourself, as well as those entrusted to you for leadership.

True leaders don't demand loyalty — they model it first, then they inspire it in others when they are seen practicing integrity, humility, and service. Before you expect loyalty from others, ask yourself the following questions:

> Have I been loyal to God's leadership assignment?

> Have I been faithful to the call of God?

> Have I stewarded His resources in a manner that earns the respect and loyalty of those I lead?

Stewardship Over Ownership

Ownership says, "This is mine." Stewardship says, "This belongs to God." Ownership seeks recognition. Stewardship seeks responsibility. Ownership is prideful. Stewardship is humble.

> *"God resists the proud but gives grace to the humble."*
>
> — James 4:6 NKJV

Leadership is an act of grace. The moment we start thinking we own the idea, we step out from under God's favor. Why? Because this posture potentially activates an inner pride that boosts our ego, thereby stealing God's glory for ourselves. This theft is generally an inadvertent byproduct of thinking that success was a direct result of our own activities and strategies.

When that happens, we run the risk of taking the credit for what God did *through* us as His instruments. After all, it's not the trumpet, but the trumpeter who makes beautiful music. Without the trumpeter, the horn would sit silently in its case. As faith-based leaders we're the trumpet, but God is the Trumpeter.

For leaders who silently wrestle with pride, many of us are adept at hiding this inward sense of overinflated self-importance from others. We give off all the outward indications of humility, but lest we forget, *"man looks at the outward appearance, but the LORD looks at the heart "*(1 Samuel 16:7 NKJV). Certainly, He knows exactly how deeply pride runs within the us.

Stewardship reminds us that leadership is a temporary trust with eternal consequences. The title you carry is just a tool God uses to impact others during your leadership tenure. At some point, your season will expire, and there will be someone else to carry the title that once made you feel so important.

Your goal is not to be remembered for what you built, but for how faithfully you managed what He entrusted to you. In the end, the true recognition and the only meaningful reward is to hear those cherished words from heaven on high when the Lord declares *"Well done, good and faithful servant; you have been faithful over a few things, I will make you ruler over many things. Enter into the joy of your lord."* (Matthew 25:21,23 NKJV)

This is why I've always felt rather uncomfortable being celebrated for my accomplishments in ministry, business, and community service. I understand why people would honor faithful leaders. It's wonderful to recognize those who serve well and let them know their efforts are appreciated.

But I also know myself, and my silent struggle with pride. Therefore, whenever I receive even the smallest compliment, my response is always a kind "thank you" followed immediately by "but all glory and honor belong to God for this accomplishment." This is to remind them of who is worthy to be praised, and to constantly remind myself to decrease and so that He may increase (John 3:30 NKJV).

The Steward's Mindset

Faithful leaders think differently. They ask:

• "How can I serve better?" instead of "How can I be seen more?"
• "What's best for the mission?" instead of "What benefits me the most?"
• "What does God want?" instead of "What do I want?"

Faithful leadership isn't about the position you hold; it's about the principles you uphold. The most powerful leaders aren't necessarily the loudest ones — they're the ones whose character quietly earns respect. That's the difference between being impressive and being impactful.

I recall early in my pastoral ministry feeling an overwhelming sense to have all the answers, meet everyone's needs, and solve everyone's problems. I thought I was "doing ministry". In my mind, I was making my calling and election sure (2 Peter 1:10 NKJV). We had a small start-up church that attracted people with a myriad of social, financial, relationship, and even criminal hardships. They all came to me looking for answers, hope, and solutions.

But beneath my good intentions was something far less noble. Ungodly pride and human arrogance convinced me that I could bear what only God was meant to carry. Instead of leading them to the true Shepherd, I tried to uphold my duties as the under shepherd, the counselor, the provider, and the fixer of all things.

So, I feverishly—and futilely—worked to solve everyone's problems. It was a hero complex dressed up as ministry, and it yielded no fruit. They didn't get the help they needed, and I ultimately burned out.

I didn't realize what was happening inside me. Pride whispered that I should be able to handle it. Fear whispered that I had to. I didn't want to disappoint God or the people He sent, so I pushed myself to be overly attentive to their needs. I took on burdens I was never meant to carry and tried to uphold an image of what I believed a pastor should be.

But it was foolish striving. It produced no real help for them and only exhaustion for me. What I didn't see at the time was this: ministry and leadership done in my own strength is still pride, even when it looks like service.

Character Is the True Currency

In every field — from construction sites to boardrooms — character will always outlast charisma. Charisma can attract a crowd. Character builds a community. People may follow your talent for a while, but they'll trust your integrity for a lifetime.

I've seen leaders rise fast because of skill and fall faster because of scandals. But faithful leaders understand this: your gift can take you places but your character must be strong enough to keep you there.

That's why faithful leadership isn't measured by how impressive you appear, but by how dependable you are when no one is watching.

Trustworthiness is the quiet strength that stabilizes everything else — your relationships, your influence, your legacy.

People don't just want a leader they admire; they want a reliable leader. And reliability comes with consistency, honesty, and the courage to be the same person in private that you are in public.

Faithful leadership isn't about being successful — it's about being trustworthy. At the end of the day, people might submit to your leadership because of your talent, but if they have doubts about your trustworthiness, they'll repossess their submissiveness, quietly withdraw from you, and leave in search of more trustworthy leadership elsewhere.

Trust is the currency of faith-based leadership. It's earned slowly, must be guarded carefully, and spent wisely. A leader who is steady, honest, and accountable will outlast the one who is flashy, unpredictable, or self-promoting. The stewardship philosophy is the glue that holds it all together.

Stewardship is Revealed Through Servant Leadership

Jesus flipped leadership upside down. He redefined greatness — not by how many people serve you, but by how many people you serve.

"Whoever desires to become great among you, let him be your servant."

— Matthew 20:26 NKJV

That doesn't mean leaders shouldn't have authority. It means authority is meant to be used for service, not status. When you lead as a servant, you start to measure success differently. You measure progress not just by profits, but by people — how they grow, how they flourish, how they feel seen and valued under your leadership. Servant leaders lift others, even when no one's lifting them.

> *"For even the Son of Man did not come to be served, but to serve, and to give His life a ransom for many"*

> Mark 10:45 NKJV

Jesus Himself redefined leadership by anchoring it in service, not superiority. If the One who had all authority in heaven and earth chose to express that authority through humility, compassion, and sacrificial love, then every faith-oriented earthly leader is called to do the same. Servant leadership isn't weakness; it's divine strength under control. It's the willingness to go low so others can rise, to step back so others can step forward.

Servant leaders understand that authority is a stewardship trust, as well, and not a spotlight. It's not given to pompously promote the leader. It's given to elevate the people. When others look to you as their leader, they should feel safer, covered, and empowered to grow. They should sense stability at all levels, not superiority reigning down on them from above.

True influence grows because your character earns it over time. And the more you reflect the heart of Christ in how you lead, the more your team, your church, or your company becomes a place where people can thrive and prosper, because they've bought into the mission as influenced by your leadership.

Faithfulness in the Little Things

Everybody wants the big win — the contract, the platform, the breakthrough. But real success is forged in the small, daily acts of disciplined faithfulness.

My college basketball coach, Darrell Halloran, used to tell us: *"Everyone wants to win, but very few people are willing to prepare to win because they ignore the little things that matter most."* That truth has stuck with me for life. It's not just about sports — it's about stewardship. Great businesses, ministries, and families aren't built on one big moment; they're built on a thousand small ones.

Showing up on time. Honoring your commitments. Returning calls promptly. Paying attention to details on a job site. Doing your paperwork accurately. And submitting reports in a timely manner are just a few examples of the seemingly small tasks that yield big results. The world celebrates the highlight reel, but God honors your faithfulness over small things.

Doing Small Better means understanding how you handle the small assignments prepares you for the big ones.

Daily habits. Daily discipline. These are the quiet rhythms that shape the kind of leader you become when no one is applauding. Big opportunities don't come simply because you prayed for them. They arrive because you prepared for them like you were expecting them.

Excellence is never an accident; it is the cumulative effect of consistent, intentional choices made day by day. When you practice discipline in small things, you build the muscle to steward the greater things.

God promotes leaders who can be trusted in the unseen moments, because what you do privately ultimately reveals who you truly are publicly. Small disciplines create strong leaders, and strong leaders create lasting impact.

Why Small Matters

Small things create momentum. The little actions may not garner headlines, but they build trust, discipline, and excellence. And excellence compounds. Just like compound interest grows wealth over time, compounding faithfulness grows influence, reputation, and opportunity.

That's why great leaders don't wait for big moments to show greatness — they practice greatness in the ordinary. Every text returned, every job done right the first time, every honest conversation, every detail double-checked becomes a seed. And seeds don't look powerful in the moment, but over time they transform landscapes.

The leader who tends to the small things with diligence becomes the leader God can trust with greater responsibility. Momentum doesn't come from miracles; it comes from consistency.

And here's the beauty of compound faithfulness: it works even when no one notices. You may not see immediate results. You may not get applause or recognition. But every act of integrity strengthens your foundation. Every disciplined choice sharpens your character.

Over time, God opens doors for leaders who have mastered the quiet work of being faithful. Influence built on charisma may crumble, but influence built on consistency endures through seasons, storms, and scrutiny.

Faithfulness Builds Capacity

When you prove you can handle the small, God can trust you with the big. Too many people pray for greater opportunities without being faithful where they are. But God's promotion always follows proven stewardship.

Think about David. Before he killed Goliath, he was faithful in the fields tending sheep. Before he became king, he delivered bread and cheese to his brothers. Faithfulness in small assignments prepared him for greater ones. How you handle small duties foreshadows your handling of bigger responsibilities when they come your way.

Doing Small Better on the Job Site

I once inspected a job site where a subcontractor had done solid work, but left debris scattered everywhere. When I asked why, he said, "It's just trash; it doesn't matter." But it did matter. That mess told the client everything they needed to know about his standards.

Excellence in small details — clean workspaces, neat finishes, careful inspections — speaks volumes about your character and your company. Clients may not always understand your technical skills, but they always notice your standards. In leadership and life, the small things aren't small. They're indicators of how seriously or cavalierly you take stewardship.

The Compounding Effect of Small Decisions

Doing Small Better isn't about perfection — it's about consistency. Every small decision is a brick. Lay enough bricks, and you build a wall. Lay enough walls, and you build a house. Lay enough houses, and you build a city.

The world celebrates big wins. God honors steady faithfulness. And in the long run, steady faithfulness always outlasts flashy shortcuts.

Practical Takeaways

1. Excellence in Details – Don't dismiss the little things; they're what people remember most.
2. Faithful Habits – Show up on time, follow through, and keep your commitments.
3. Short-Term Sacrifice, Long-Term Gain – A hundred small faithful actions will bring greater reward than one lucky break.
4. Servant Leadership – Measure success by how you lift others, not how

high you rise.

5. Integrity Over Image – Build credibility through consistency; reputation will follow.

Reflection & Action Steps

1. Redefine Success: Write down what success means to you — not according to the world, but according to God's Word.

2. Assess Your Motives: Ask yourself: Am I managing God's assignment, or am I trying to own it?

3. Serve Intentionally: Identify one person this week you can serve without expectation — simply because it honors God.

4. Pray for Humility: Ask God to keep you mindful that every resource, relationship, and opportunity is His.

5. Do Small Better: Choose one area of your daily routine to raise your standard of excellence this week.

Closing Thoughts...

Doing Small Better isn't just a catchy phrase — it's a Kingdom principle. Faithful leadership isn't about being celebrated; it's about being credible. It's about doing what's right when no one's clapping, staying consistent when no one's watching, and trusting God when no one's understanding.

Don't despise small beginnings. Celebrate them. Steward them. Because in God's economy, the small things are what open the door to greater things.

Chapter 3

Ethics- The Foundation of Faith-Based Leadership

"Therefore, whatever you want men to do to you, do also to them, for this is the Law and the Prophets."

Matthew 7:12 NKJV

The Foundation Beneath It All

Every lasting structure depends on what lies beneath it. It's no secret that a building is only as good as the foundation upon which it's built. No matter how esthetically pleasing a house appears, if it sits on a compromised foundation, instability is inevitable.

Cracks eventually emerge in the walls—quiet at first, hidden in the shadows, but relentlessly spreading until they can no longer be ignored. If the foundation is really poor, in time, the entire structure may lean, sag, or collapse under the weight of its own design.

The same principle applies to faith-based leadership. Leadership built on talent may rise quickly, but leadership built on ethics stands the tests of time. While talent may elevate you, ethics will sustain you. Sound, godly leadership is built on a strong ethical foundation.

You cannot construct a ministry, business, or organization on weak moral footing and expect God to put His hand of blessing upon it. You can preach purpose, declare vision, and recite scripture, but if the foundation beneath it all is ethically unstable, the structure will not stand—not spiritually, not practically, and certainly not long-term.

God is not obligated to prosper what we build on compromised character. If the motives are wrong, the methods questionable, or the standards inconsistent, the poor foundation will eventually reveal the truth.

Even Christianity had to be built on a sure foundation. Scripture declares, *"For no other foundation can anyone lay than that which is laid, which is Jesus Christ"* (1 Corinthians 3:11). If our very faith requires a firm foundation, then the leadership we practice in His name requires the same. Faith-based leadership is not merely leadership sprinkled with scripture; it is leadership anchored in Christ-like ethics that guide behavior, decisions, and culture.

But ethical leadership does not come by accident. One of the greatest challenges for faith-based leaders today is navigating a secular world with spiritual conviction. We live in a culture where morals shift like sand and values are determined by convenience rather than conviction.

Titles don't provide clarity. Credentials don't provide clarity. Experience doesn't provide clarity. Not even passion provides clarity. Ethical standards provide clarity.

Ethical standards answer the questions every faith-based leader must confront:

1. How will I lead?

2. What will I tolerate?

3. What will I refuse?

4. What will I stand for?

5. How will I stand when it costs me something?

In a world where truth is relative and morality is flexible, ethical standards anchor the leader to something deeper and more meaningful. They become a compass, pointing toward righteousness when pressure attempts to bend your integrity. They guide you through seasons of conflict, decision-making, success, failure, criticism, opportunity, and temptation. They keep you grounded when your influence grows and when the applause of men threatens to get louder than the voice of God.

Faith-based leaders cannot assume they have ethics simply because they have faith. Faith does not automatically produce ethical clarity. Conviction must be defined. Character must be shaped. Standards must be written and communicated. Why? Because undefined ethics eventually become *optional* ethics, and optional ethics can lead to three problems:

1. It leaves the door open to possible corruption
2. It produces inconsistent leadership
3. It creates an unstable culture

Bottom line? Whatever is not clearly defined could be easily compromised. I was taught as a child to stand for something or risk falling for anything. Core values and ethical standards give you something solid to stand on when everything around you is unpredictable.

Before ethics can guide an organization, they must govern the leader. A ministry, business, or church will never rise above the ethical standard of the ones leading it. If the leader cuts corners, the people will too. If the leader stretches the truth, the culture will normalize deception. If the leader lacks consistency or humility, the environment will absorb those traits just as quickly.

Ethics must be lived privately before they can be trusted publicly. A leader's integrity in quiet places determines whether their influence can withstand the weight of public responsibility and scrutiny.

Jesus as the Ethical Model

Every faith-based ethical standard ultimately traces back to Jesus Himself. Jesus didn't just teach ethics—He embodied them. His life is the clearest picture of ethical leadership the world has ever seen.

He respected the dignity of every person He encountered. He spoke truth even when it was unpopular. He exemplified excellence in His obedience to the Father. He took responsibility for sins He didn't even commit. He showed compassion to the hurting, fairness to the marginalized, and citizenship in how He served the world He came to save.

Jesus showed us that ethics aren't just rules—they are reflection.

> Ethical leadership reflects His character.
> Ethical conduct reflects His nature.
> Ethical decisions reflect His heart.

If Jesus is the model, then ethics are not optional for leaders who claim His name. They are the natural overflow of following Him.

When Ethical Standards Are Ignored

When ethics are ignored, leadership becomes dangerous. Without ethical boundaries, power becomes intoxicating, influence becomes manipulative, decisions become self-serving, the culture invites toxicity, teams experience division, vision gets blurred, and leaders become like demigods.

Unethical leadership may appear to work for a season—drawing crowds, producing results, or generating revenue—but eventually cracks appear in the foundation. And when the foundation fails, everything built upon it collapses.

Unethical leadership inevitably breaks down morally, relationally, financially, or spiritually. Organizations rarely fail because of weak mission statements; they fail because of weak moral foundations.

History is full of reminders that when ethics are ignored, even the most successful organizations eventually collapse under the weight of their own poor character.

Enron was once one of the most admired companies in America, yet it crumbled because deception became more valuable than integrity. WorldCom disintegrated after an $11 billion accounting scandal. Theranos unraveled when their promises were exposed as lies. Wells Fargo damaged decades of credibility by opening millions of fraudulent accounts to inflate performance. Volkswagen paid billions in fines for cheating emissions tests. FTX imploded when billions in customer funds were misused. And Lehman Brothers triggered a global financial crisis by valuing profit over responsibility.

Just as the business world offers sobering examples of organizations that collapsed under compromised ethics, the Church has faced its own painful failures.

The PTL Club and Heritage USA crumbled after financial misconduct and moral scandal shattered public trust. The Crystal Cathedral fell into bankruptcy following years of financial mismanagement and internal conflict. Entire dioceses within the Catholic Church suffered catastrophic loss of credibility after decades of abuse and systemic cover-ups were exposed.

More recently, Hillsong—once considered one of the most influential global ministries—experienced widespread resignations, campus closures, and public fallout due to moral failure, financial opacity, and unhealthy leadership culture.

These tragedies span denominations, countries, and theological backgrounds, yet they all reveal the same familiar patterns: leaders operated without accountability, systems favored secrecy over transparency, image became more important than integrity, organizational loyalty replaced moral responsibility, and correction was resisted instead of welcomed.

In every case, ethical failure preceded the organizational failure. The collapse was spiritual long before it became structural. These organizations did not fail because of weak strategies, weak talent, or weak mission statements—they failed because their leaders abandoned ethical integrity.

Skills can expand an organization, but only ethics can sustain it.

The Visual Framework:
Foundation → Compass → Culture → Leadership

FOUNDATION
Ethics form the base. Without a solid ethical foundation, nothing built on top can endure.

COMPASS
Ethical standards direct decisions. They orient the leader toward truth when pressure, temptation, or confusion attempt to distort judgment.

CULTURE
Ethical consistency shapes organizational identity.
What the leader models becomes what the team normalizes.

LEADERSHIP
Ethical leadership produces credibility, trust, influence, and long-term sustainability. Ethical clarity strengthens leaders for the long haul.

Leadership is not just what you build— it's what you build *on*.

That's why I created what I call **The Super Seven Ethical Standards**—seven timeless principles I have personally learned to lead by in business and ministry. They are simple, scriptural, and strong enough to withstand any cultural storm.

The Super Seven are as follows:

RESPECT

HONESTY

EXCELLENCE

RESPONSIBILITY

COMPASSION

FAIRNESS

CITIZENSHIP

They are not just values, they are commitments. Not just ideals, they are practices. Not just beliefs, they are behaviors.

I highly recommend that every faith-based leader identifies and adopts a set of written, clearly communicated ethical standards that are non-negotiable. These standards will become your spiritual compass and guide you through the complexities of leading with faith in a secular world.

You may or may not adopt my Super Seven, but in the chapters that follow, I invite you to examine them deeply. Let them challenge you. Let them refine you. Let them strengthen your leadership. Because ethical standards are not a side note to leadership—they are the substance of it. They are the foundation beneath it all.

Chapter 4

Respect- The Culture Creator of Faith-based Leadership

"Therefore, whatever you want men to do to you, do also to them, for this is the Law and the Prophets."

--Matthew 7:12 NKJV

Respect is more than courtesy. It is the recognition of God-given value in every person you lead, serve, or work alongside. When respect is present, relationships strengthen, communication is clearer, and unity becomes attainable.

When respect is absent, even skilled teams struggle to function because respect doesn't begin with skill. It begins with a heart that sees value in other people regardless of what or how much they bring to the proverbial "table".

Every leader must decide what they truly believe about people. Are they assets? Are they obstacles? Are they tools to accomplish your goals? Or are they individuals made in the image of God, entrusted to your care? Philippians 2:3 NKJV says *"Let nothing be done through selfish ambition or conceit, but in lowliness of mind let each esteem others better than himself."*

To "esteem others" is to elevate their significance — to treat people with dignity, care, and humility. Respect is not a reaction to how people behave, but rather a reflection of who you are as a leader in relation to others, despite their behavior. This ethical standard does not just shape culture—it creates culture.

Respect is not theoretical. It's highly practical and pragmatic. It shows up in the small, daily behaviors that communicate honor:

- Listening without interrupting
- Being punctual and prepared
- Giving clear, consistent communication
- Recognizing contributions publicly and privately
- Correcting without humiliating

- Treating disagreements as conversations, not confrontations
- Keeping your word even when it costs you
- Allow concerns to be raised without fear of retribution
- Make volunteers feel appreciated, not used
- Encourage people to grow without being belittled for their shortcomings
- Address differences without creating division

These are often referred to as "soft skills." But I believe they're deeper than you think. I've come to realize that most people are more feeling-oriented than they are logical, and that creating an environment where they *feel* respected is becoming increasingly more essential to effective leadership than ever before.

When people feel respected, they work with greater focus and greater commitment. They show up with energy, initiative, and loyalty. But even the most gifted person will withdraw when they feel dismissed, disrespected, or unappreciated.

One person who feels respected and aligned with the mission will outperform three highly capable people who show up out of obligation but secretly wish they were somewhere else. In addition, people who feel respected and appreciated are more likely to promote team unity.

Unity in a small organization is essential because losing just one or two good people can be crushing. And just as dangerous, one dissatisfied person in the camp can spread negativity and create dissension that takes on a life of its own. In a small team, this kind of destructive influence has a faster, deeper, and more damaging impact than it would in a larger group.

Small churches and small businesses can't always blame their struggles on the hardships of performing the mission. Sometimes, they struggle because of the way they deal with people. When people feel dishonored, unheard, or dismissed, teamwork declines and turnover increases.

The truth is simple: people don't abandon healthy organizations—they leave disrespectful environments shaped by leaders who either disregard or downplay the importance of creating a respectful culture.

As I look back on my tenure as a pastor, I can see moments where my leadership fell short in this area. I didn't recognize it at the time, but with growth, maturity, and a few gray hairs, I now understand that some of my well-intentioned actions might have still communicated disrespect.

For example, in my zeal for contemporary expression, I overlooked the emotional weight and personal significance some of the church traditions had on people. I unintentionally offended people who were among the most genuine, loving, and supportive members of our church family. My heart was in the right place, but my execution could have been better.

Sure, many of my initiatives were fruitful, but at what expense? Did curating a new environment require making some people feel devalued? I don't think so. There was probably a more respectful way to achieve the same result. I understand that no matter what you do, some people will be offended. However, I firmly believe that moments like that can still be managed respectfully.

Practical Takeaways

1. Respect begins with recognizing the God-given value in every person you lead.

2. Culture is shaped daily through practical behaviors: listening well, communicating clearly, and keeping your word.

3. People often respond more to how they feel than to what they hear, making respectful environments essential.

4. One respected, mission-aligned person is more valuable than several skilled but disengaged individuals.

5. Many small organizations struggle not because of mission, but because of how people are treated.

Reflection & Action Steps

1. Identify one behavior you practice that communicates respect — and one that may unintentionally communicate disrespect.

2. Choose one person this week to intentionally honor, encourage, or listen to more deeply.

3. Evaluate whether your team feels safe raising concerns without fear of retribution.

4. Reflect on a past decision where zeal may have overshadowed sensitivity and identify what you can learn from it.

5. Commit to one practical action this week that strengthens a culture of respect in your organization.

Closing Thoughts...

Respect is not just one of the Super Seven Ethical Standards — it is the relational glue that holds them all together. Integrity demands respect. Accountability requires respect. Humility expresses respect. Excellence reflects respect.

- Where respect is practiced, people flourish.
- Where respect is absent, organizations fracture.
- Respect is the foundation that allows every other leadership virtue to thrive.

Chapter 5

Honesty- The Trust Builder of Faith-based Leadership

"Lying lips are an abomination to the Lord, but those who deal truthfully are His delight."

-Proverbs 12:22 NKJV

Honesty is the alignment of your words, your actions, and your intentions. Leaders who deal honestly build trust, and trust is the invisible glue that holds relationships, teams, and entire organizations together. Whether you're talking about soldiers in battle, athletes in competition, or believers building genuine community, trust is the nonnegotiable ingredient of winning teamwork.

When people are confident in the honesty and integrity of their leaders—and convinced that their teammates are as committed to the mission as they are—collective strength emerges. Trust multiplies effort and allows a team to achieve together what none of them could accomplish alone.

Deception may offer a temporary advantage, but it always produces long-term loss. The faithful leader understands this, choosing honesty over convenience and declaring, "I'd rather lose a deal with integrity than win one with deception." As a contractor, this is all too real for me.

When I first started doing insurance repairs, I was presented with an enticing proposition. A homeowner wanted to collect the insurance money with no intention of ever repairing the house. He wanted me to complete and submit all the paperwork to the adjuster, and when the funds arrived, he would pay me a handsome "commission" simply for doing the paperwork.

I said no. The money was tempting, but the compromise was too costly. It was dishonest and unethical. It's insurance fraud, and the last time I checked, insurance fraud was illegal. Taking that money would've done more than violate the law, it would've violated my conscience!

The crazy part is that he knew I was a pastor. Could you imagine if I had taken that deal? My local reputation could've been tarnished, my witness for Christ could've been voided, and the members of our church might have heard how their pastor talks the talk it but doesn't walk the walk. No deal. I walked away with my head held high.

Honesty isn't weakness. It's wisdom. Weak leaders hide behind excuses, half-truths, and selective storytelling because they fear how the truth will make them look. Wise leaders understand that truth may be uncomfortable, but it is always constructive when spoken in love and seasoned with grace. Honesty is not an excuse for harshness.

Scripture calls leaders to *"speak the truth in love"* (Ephesians 4:15 NKJV). Truth without love becomes brutality, and love without truth becomes passivity. Healthy leadership requires both. When truth is delivered with compassion, clarity, and grace, people can receive correction without feeling condemned. That's a leader you can trust.

Honesty requires courage, clarity, and character. When you choose honesty, you may lose a momentary advantage, but you gain long-term credibility. When you choose honesty, you may disappoint someone temporarily, but you strengthen the relationship over time.

Weakness avoids truth to protect an image. Wisdom embraces truth to build integrity. Choosing honesty is choosing the path that God can bless and people can follow.

Honesty must become a lifestyle, not a moment. Anyone can tell the truth when it's easy, but the true test comes when telling the truth costs you something. Being honest isn't merely about avoiding lies; it's about refusing to mislead, manipulate, exaggerate, conceal vital information, or present half-truths.

Dishonesty creates illusions. Honesty embraces reality. Leadership demands courage, and honesty is simply courage expressed through transparency.

Truth simplifies leadership. Dishonesty complicates everything. When leaders operate truthfully, trust grows, communication clears, and expectations become easier to understand. Teams feel safer, mistakes get acknowledged sooner, and unity is strengthened. People will forgive honest mistakes, but they rarely forgive manipulation. A single lie can undo years of credibility, while the leader committed to truth becomes a stabilizing presence.

Honesty Supports a Safe Culture

Honesty builds emotional safety, and emotional safety produces confidence in a leader's authority. A title may grant position but only trust in the person behind the title earns true influence. When people know their leader tells the truth, they stop guessing motives and start communicating openly. They stop operating out of fear and start taking initiative. But dishonesty — especially the small, subtle kind — creates suspicion, and suspicion quietly erodes momentum.

People can detect lies even when they can't fully explain them. Have you ever heard someone say "I can't put my finger on it, but something just isn't right" about a leader? Usually, it's because the leader is never held accountable for making sure their actions line up with their words.

Honesty and accountability go hand in hand. Dishonest leaders avoid accountability because accountability threatens the illusion they're trying to protect. Honest leaders welcome accountability because honesty has nothing to hide. Accountability protects your integrity, your team, and your mission. It strengthens credibility rather than diminishing it.

Humility is also inseparable from honesty. Humility acknowledges, "I don't know everything," and "I'm not always right." Pride tries to preserve an image; honesty protects character.

Leaders do not lose credibility by admitting mistakes — they lose credibility by covering them. Honesty preserves your authenticity, and humility preserves your teachability. Together, they form the character of a trustworthy leader.

Honesty Strengthens a Team

People don't simply listen to your words; they measure your consistency. Honesty restores broken trust, heals strained relationships, strengthens unity, attracts the right people, and clarifies culture. Dishonest environments make people anxious.

Honest environments make people confident. Honesty tells those you lead, "You can trust that what I say is what I mean, and you can trust where we're going." That trust becomes the foundation upon which stable, lasting leadership is built.

I learned this firsthand in my leadership journey. During one particular crisis, in my attempt to keep morale high, I softened the truth more than I should have. I didn't lie, but I didn't tell the whole truth either.

One of our quietest and most unassuming elders sensed it. He pulled me aside and said, "Pastor, I don't need everything to be perfect. I just need to know I can trust what you're saying." Those words had deep and meaningful impact.

I realized then that half-truths from a leader create whole insecurities in the followers. People don't need perfect leaders — they need honest leaders.

That week, I gathered the entire team, laid out the real picture, and left nothing hidden. Instead of losing confidence, they leaned in. Instead of fear, unity arose. Instead of hiding problems, we tackled them together. Honesty didn't weaken the team — it strengthened it. It reminded me that truth doesn't just inform people; it empowers them.

Practical Takeaways

1. Honesty is a lifestyle that requires courage, consistency, and clarity.

2. Honesty simplifies leadership. Dishonesty complicates it.

3. Even small lies can erode credibility, influence, and unity.

4. Honesty, humility and accountability work together to build trust.

5. Honest leadership creates emotionally safety environments.

Reflection & Action Steps

1. Identify one area where you may avoid full honesty and commit to addressing it.

2. Ask a trusted team member if any of your communication feels unclear or incomplete.

3. Reflect on a moment when honesty cost you something and what it taught you.

4. Evaluate whether your culture feels safe enough for people to tell you the truth.

5. Take one action this week that reinforces honesty — clarify, correct, or confess.

Closing Thoughts...

Honesty is more than telling the truth — it is becoming the kind of leader who can be trusted with truth. It means choosing clarity over convenience, integrity over image, and vulnerability over self-preservation. A dishonest environment may grow quickly, but it cannot grow strong. A truthful environment may grow slowly, but it will grow with stability. God delights in truth, and the people you lead depend on it.

Chapter 6

Excellence – The Trademark of Faith-based Leadership

"Whatever you do, do it heartily, as to the Lord and not to men."

-*Colossians 3:23 NKJV*

Excellence is the result of doing ordinary things extraordinarily well because you know Who you're doing them for. You may not be the best, but you are committed to doing the best you can with what God has placed in your hands. When you consistently offer your best, excellence becomes your trademark because it shows that you care about what God thinks of your effort.

Excellence isn't about impressing people; it's about honoring God through the quality of your work, the integrity of your actions, and the stewardship of your responsibilities.

Excellence Begins in the Heart

Excellence must be an internal decision long before it becomes an external action. It begins with a heartfelt conviction that everything you touch should reflect the character of the God you serve. It isn't motivated by applause; it's motivated by acknowledging that God favored you by giving you the assignment. Realize that He could've chosen someone else, but He chose you. That alone is worth honoring Him with an excellent offering.

Excellence is less about outdoing others and more about outdoing the lesser version of yourself that would have surely given less than your best effort. When excellence becomes part of your core values, it flows naturally into how you serve, how you lead, and how you represent Christ in the marketplace.

People don't just see excellence; they can feel it because it has energy. It has rhythm. They see it in the details you don't skip. They feel it in the corners you refuse to cut. And they recognize the standards you refuse to lower. Excellence is not loud, but it is quietly consistent. And that consistency is a testament to the trustworthiness of your leadership.

Excellence Everyday

Excellence reveals itself through daily habits, not through dramatic moments. It's found in:

- Showing up prepared
- Finishing what you start
- Following through on promises
- Communicating clearly
- Maintaining order and structure
- Paying attention to the details others overlook
- Delegating tasks to others and supporting their efforts

Excellence is not a once-in-a-while push. It's a standard operating procedure. And because it's built on discipline rather than emotion, it remains steady even when motivation fades. Small improvements, done faithfully, become major outcomes over time. Excellence compounds because when you do the small things well over time, God begins trusting you with greater things.

Excellence Communicates Value

People interpret your level of care as your level of respect. Excellence says, *"You matter enough for me to give my best."* Whether it's a sermon, a contract proposal, a business meeting, a construction project, a sales presentation, or a simple text message, people can tell the difference between something you rushed and something you prepared.

Excellence is not about perfection — it's about intention. And intention is how you say, without words, *"I value this enough to give my all."* It annoys the living daylights out of me to watch a gifted or talented person go through the motions with a careless attitude. I'd rather see a person of less skill give it all they've got. I can cheer for that person. I'm willing to help someone with that attitude.

When leaders model excellence, teams rise to that standard. When leaders tolerate mediocrity, mediocrity becomes the culture. Your level of excellence sets the pace for everyone who follows you.

Legendary Championship NFL Coach Mike Shannahan became well known for the phrase *"never accept in a win what you wouldn't accept in a loss"*. For many coaches and players, a win is a win, no matter how you get it. With that attitude they're willing to overlook sloppy play, turnovers, lackluster effort, etc.

Shanahan was different. He was more critical of his team after a win than he was a loss. He meticulously scoured through game film looking for every little flaw. Every seemingly meaningless mistake was pointed out and corrected in practice the following week.

At first it seemed overbearing, but eventually everyone in the organization adopted his philosophy because he consistently modeled the attitude of excellence. The result? Back-to-back Superbowl victories.

That same mindset applies to business, leadership, and ministry. Too many people overlook the small things and then wonder why they don't win. They want winning results without embracing the discipline of mundane, repetitive, detail-focused work. Excellence isn't built in the spotlight — it's built in the unglamorous shadows of preparation.

Accountability: The Key to Leadership Excellence

Excellence requires accountability because it doesn't flourish in isolation. Excellence grows where feedback is welcomed, not avoided. Excellence has a posture that says, *"Help me get better. Show me where I can improve. Hold me to the standard I've committed to."*

People who pursue excellence don't fear evaluation, they embrace it. They understand that growth demands feedback, and that receiving feedback demands humility.

Excellence is a journey, not a destination, and the moment a leader stops getting better is the moment they begin to fall behind. True excellence invites sharpening, correction, and refinement because it knows that stagnation is the enemy of leadership growth. Excellence understands that growth is never a solo pursuit—God designed us to be shaped in community.

"As iron sharpens iron, so a man sharpens the countenance of his friend."
-Proverbs 27:17 NKJV

Iron cannot sharpen itself, and neither can a leader. It takes friction, honest conversation, and trusted voices to bring out our best. Sharpening moments may feel uncomfortable, but they are essential to your development. When we surround ourselves with people who challenge us, refine us, and refuse to let us settle for mediocrity, we position ourselves to grow with strength and integrity.

Excellence is cultivated in relationships where truth is spoken, blind spots are revealed, and character is strengthened. It is in that sharpening process that God forms leaders whose excellence reflects His glory.

"Faithful are the wounds of a friend, but the kisses of an enemy are deceitful."
-Proverbs 27:6 NKJV

Accountability is not always comfortable, but it is always necessary. True friends and true leaders love you enough to tell you what you need to hear, not just what you want to hear. Their correction may sting for a moment, but it strengthens your character and protects your calling.

Flattery is easy and often deceptive, but honest feedback—given in love—helps refine the areas where excellence needs to grow. Excellence welcomes these trusted voices because it recognizes that faithful wounds heal, while deceitful kisses harm. And when you allow the right people to speak truth into your life, you position yourself to rise into the level of leadership excellence God intended for you.

Excellence Honors God and Earns Influence

When you lead with excellence, you don't just stand out — you stand apart. Excellence opens doors, builds influence, and establishes a good name. Proverbs 22:1 reminds us that *"a good name is to be chosen rather than great riches."* A good name is built on consistent excellence.

Excellence also amplifies your witness. People may not remember every sermon you preach or every product you deliver, but they'll remember the spirit of excellence behind it. Excellence reflects the God you represent.

Practical Takeaway

1. Excellence is a commitment to honoring God with your best.
2. Small daily habits — preparation, clarity, consistency — create a culture of excellence.
3. Excellence communicates value.
4. Accountability strengthens excellence by exposing blind spots and encouraging growth.
5. Excellence earns trust, expands influence, and reflects the character of Christ.

Reflection & Action Steps

1. Identify one area where your standards have slipped and re-commit to excellence in that area.
2. Ask a trusted person where your leadership could become more consistent or refined.
3. Reflect on a recent task: Did your level of preparation reflect your values?
4. Choose one daily habit (organization, preparation, punctuality, follow-through) to strengthen this week.
5. Set a visible standard of excellence that your team or ministry can follow and model consistently.

Closing Thoughts…

Excellence is not about being the best of the best. It's about doing the best with what you have. It is the discipline of presenting God with work that honors Him and presenting people with leadership that blesses them. Excellence is the signature of stewardship. When you commit to excellence, you honor your calling, strengthen your credibility, and expand your influence. Excellence says to God, *"I'm grateful for what You've given me,"* and it says to people, *"You're worth the effort."*

Chapter 7

Responsibility – The Weight of Faith-based Leadership

"To whom much is given, much will be required."

— *Luke 12:48 NKJV*

Responsibility is the quiet weight every leader carries, whether they acknowledge it or not. It is the realization that what God places in your hands, He expects you to steward with diligence, integrity, and faithfulness.

Responsibility isn't simply about completing tasks — it's about owning your role in the process that produces outcomes. It's about recognizing that God didn't entrust you with influence, people, opportunities, or resources by accident.

Leadership is never given for comfort; it is given for purpose. And responsibility is the price we pay in pursuit of that purpose.

Responsibility means you don't blame, excuse, or pass the burden along to someone else. You recognize that leadership demands that someone responds — not just to victories, but to mistakes, missteps, and missed opportunities. Responsibility says, *"If it is in my hands, it is under my care."* And God honors leaders who take responsibility seriously.

A Responsibility State of Mind

Responsibility is a sober-minded awareness that God has entrusted you with something that matters — people, influence, resources, time, gifting, or opportunity. This mindset shifts leadership from casual to consecrated. It moves you from seeing your role as something you *do* to seeing it as something you have been entrusted with overseeing.

Casual leadership treats responsibility lightly, but consecrated leadership treats it as sacred stewardship. When you understand that God placed you in your position on purpose, your decisions carry more weight, your actions carry more intention, and your service carries more reverence.

It isn't motivated by pressure; it's motivated by gratitude. Responsibility recognizes, *"God didn't have to choose me, but He did."* That divine trust should ignite a sense of holy obligation to handle your assignment with excellence, integrity, and care. A responsible leader expresses gratitude because they understand that every assignment is both a privilege and a gift from God, and gratitude fuels the desire to steward that gift well.

A responsible leader doesn't need to be reminded, pushed, or supervised. They're proactive. They're intentional. They move with initiative. They follow through. They finish what they start. And because responsibility is part of their core values, it naturally flows into how they lead, how they serve, and how they represent Christ in doing so.

Responsibility Everyday

Responsibility is not demonstrated in grand gestures — it's revealed in daily habits. It shows up in:

- Doing what you said you would do
- Taking initiative instead of waiting for instruction
- Following through on commitments
- Admitting mistakes without excuses
- Being faithful with small tasks
- Owning the need to provide resolutions to problems

Responsibility is not about feeling inspired all the time. It doesn't rise and fall with circumstances. It stands firm because it's anchored in conviction rather than convenience. In fact, most of the time responsibility is accompanied by tremendous inconvenience. Being responsible requires time, attention, and resources that can cost you quite a bit.

As a state licensed residential contractor, things don't always work out as planned. Responsible leadership means owning your part in the process that produced the situation at hand—especially when things don't go according to plan.

In my line of work, projects don't always unfold the way they were designed on paper. Materials fail, timelines shift, and sometimes people make mistakes. But when something goes wrong, I don't blame my guys, point fingers, or hide behind excuses. I take responsibility. I confront the issue head-on, fix the problem, and make the client whole, even if it costs more than I planned or budgeted for.

There have been times when I absorbed the entire financial loss—not because I had to, but because my integrity required it. I've walked away from jobs in the red, but I walked away with something money can't buy: a good name. And in leadership, a good name is worth more than any profit margin.

Responsible leaders protect their reputation by honoring their word, owning up to their mistakes, and doing whatever it takes to make things right. Whenever you steward the small things well by being responsible, God prepares you for the larger responsibilities ahead. He elevates those He trusts to handle more to greater assignments that come with greater responsibility.

Responsibility Communicates Character

People judge your character by how seriously you take your responsibilities. If a leader cannot be trusted with the small, everyday things, people will hesitate to trust them with the bigger things that matter most.

Responsibility is how you show others that you respect them, value their time, and honor your commitments. Irresponsibility communicates carelessness — and carelessness is costly.

Few things destroy confidence in leadership faster than inconsistency, excuses, or unreliability. But when people see that you consistently take responsibility for your work, your attitude, your decisions, and your words, their trust in your leadership grows stronger. Godly leadership is not just what you do when things fall nicely into place— it's what you take responsibility for when everything falls apart.

Accountability: The Partner of Responsibility

Responsibility cannot flourish without accountability. Accountability keeps you honest, grounded, and growing. Responsibility says, *"This is mine to carry,"* while accountability says, *"And I'm willing to be sharpened in the process."* Iron cannot sharpen itself. A responsible leader invites sharpening, correction, and refinement because they understand that responsibility requires humility and teachability.

Accountability may be uncomfortable, but it is essential. It protects you from blind spots. It corrects drift. It strengthens discipline. It keeps your stewardship clean before God and credible before people.

Initiative: The Mark of a Mature Leader

Mature leaders don't wait for problems to become crises before they act. They anticipate, evaluate, and initiate. They understand that true responsibility is proactive, not reactive.

A responsible leader:

- Addresses issues early
- Makes decisions prayerfully
- Confronts challenges directly
- Communicates clearly
- Protects the mission and the people involved

Avoidance, denial, and procrastination are the enemies of responsibility. Initiative is the antidote. People follow leaders who carry weight well. When they see you take responsibility, especially for the tough, uncomfortable things, your influence grows.

Responsibility Honors God and Earns Trust

Responsibility is spiritual before it is practical. It honors God because it reflects His character. God is faithful, consistent, and trustworthy, and responsible leaders should mirror those traits.

When you lead responsibly, you earn trust. Trust builds influence. Influence multiplies impact. People may forget your gifts, but they never forget your dependability. Responsibility is one of the greatest testimonies a leader can offer.

Practical Takeaways

1. Responsibility is ownership — not excuses, blame, or avoidance.
2. Small daily habits reveal your true level of responsibility.
3. Accountability and responsibility work together to strengthen leadership.
4. People trust leaders who take responsibility seriously.
5. Responsibility honors God and increases your influence among men.

Reflection & Action Steps

1. Identify one area where you've been avoiding responsibility and commit to owning it this week.
2. Evaluate your daily habits: Are you consistent, disciplined, and dependable?
3. Ask a trusted person where irresponsibility or inconsistency may be costing you influence.
4. Choose one important task you've delayed and complete it today.
5. Reflect on what God has entrusted to you — and write down how you will honor that trust moving forward.

Closing Thoughts…

Responsibility is not a burden — it is a blessing. It is God's way of saying, *"I trust you with this."* When you embrace responsibility with humility, discipline, and faithfulness, you position yourself for greater influence and deeper impact.

Responsibility is the evidence of maturity, the expression of stewardship, and the pathway to God's favor. When you carry what God placed in your hands well, He can trust you with even more.

Chapter 8

Compassion – The Heart of Faith-based Leadership

"Finally, all of you be of one mind, having compassion for one another; love as brothers, be tenderhearted, be courteous."

— *1 Peter 3:8 NKJV*

Compassion is the ethical standard that softens leadership without weakening it. It is the ability to see people not just as workers, volunteers, or followers, but as human beings with burdens, battles, and stories of their own. Compassion is not pity, but it is recognition of the unspoken issues of life that impact the day-to-day functioning of those you lead. It is the willingness to step into someone else's experience with understanding, patience, and grace. Compassion says, *"I see you. I value you. I care about what you're carrying."*

Leadership without compassion becomes cold. Leadership with compassion becomes compelling. People will work for a competent leader, but they will sacrifice for a compassionate one. Compassion creates connection, and connection builds unity — the kind of unity that makes teams stronger, churches healthier, and organizations more resilient.

Compassion Starts Within

Compassion must be an internal posture of the heart before it becomes an external practice. It begins with acknowledging that everyone is fighting battles you cannot see. The Apostle Paul wrote in Ephesians 6:12 *"For we do not wrestle against flesh and blood, but against principalities, against powers, against the rulers of the darkness of this age, against spiritual hosts of wickedness in the heavenly places."*

Compassion is rooted in empathy, but it grows through intentionality. It requires slowing down long enough to listen, observe, and care.

Compassion is motivated by gratitude. When you realize how often God has been patient, tender, and merciful toward you, it becomes much easier to extend that same grace toward others. Compassion flows naturally from a heart that remembers, *"I've received mercy, so I should demonstrate mercy."*

When compassion becomes one of your core values, it shapes how you respond to people. It influences your tone, your timing, your expectations, and your decisions. It reminds you that leadership is not just about tasks. It's about people.

People recognize compassion. They see it in your patience, your presence, and your willingness to pause for a minute to hear them out. Compassion is quiet, but it is powerful. It softens hearts and strengthens relationships.

Compassion Requires Action, Not Just Emotion

Compassion isn't merely what you feel, it's what you *do* because of what you feel. Biblical compassion is never passive. In Scripture, compassion always moves. Every time the Gospels say Jesus was *"moved with compassion,"* He acted. He fed the hungry, healed the hurting, taught the multitudes, delivered the oppressed, and restored the broken. His compassion produced movement. His heart compelled His hands.

True compassion is not sentimental, it is responsive. It steps toward people rather than away from them. It enters their struggle with intention instead of remaining a distant observer. Compassion shows up through support, service, and sacrifice.

In leadership, compassion means:

- Checking in when you know someone is struggling
- Offering help instead of waiting to be asked
- Lightening the load when you notice someone being overwhelmed
- Restoring the fallen gently rather than condemning them harshly
- Providing clarity to someone drowning in confusion

People don't feel your compassion because you say that you care. They feel it because you show that you care. They interpret that as genuine concern for their well-being. Emotion may touch the heart, but compassionate action transforms their unbearable circumstances into something a bit more manageable.

Compassion Sees Beyond Profit

Compassionate leadership is seen beyond numbers, margins, and bottom lines. Profit may measure success, but compassion measures impact. A compassionate leader understands that people are not expenses — they are partners in the work. They recognize that behind every task is a person, behind every role is a story, and behind every performance is a life being lived.

Compassion sees the human being before the human resource. Profit-driven leadership asks, *"How did you perform?"* Compassionate leadership also asks, *"How are you doing?"*

Compassion sees beyond productivity and into the person. And when people feel seen, they perform from a deeper place of commitment, loyalty, and willingness. Nevertheless, just because compassion is pro-people, it doesn't mean that it's anti-profit. It is pro-people, and when people flourish, the organization flourishes too. And it usually shows in the bottom line.

Compassion Everyday

Compassion is not expressed through grand gestures. It's revealed in daily actions. It shows up when leaders:

- Listen before speaking

- Show patience with slow learners or struggling people

- Offer grace instead of harsh criticism

- Ask questions instead of making assumptions

- Support people through personal or spiritual challenges

- Make space for humanity, not just productivity

Compassion is not weakness. It's wisdom! It does not coddle irresponsibility, but it does consider context. Compassion examines *why* before judging *what*. And in doing so, it helps people heal, grow, and rise beyond their struggles, which typically inspires them to perform better.

Leadership is never just about the mission — it's also about the people who carry out the details of the mission with you. In fact, I dare say that the people are more important than the mission, because without them the mission would simply be a concept with no hands, feet, or ingenuity to bring it to life.

Compassion Communicates Dignity

Every human being wants to feel seen, heard, and valued. Compassion communicates dignity in a way that no policy, program, or gift ever could. It tells people they are more than their mistakes, more than their productivity, and more than their role in your organization.

When a leader practices compassion, people feel safe bringing their concerns, weaknesses, and wounds. And when people feel safe, they become more honest, more committed, and more connected. Compassion builds trust because it meets people at the level of their humanity.

Harshness may produce compliance, but compassion produces commitment.

Correcting with Compassion

Compassion does not eliminate correction — it shapes the way correction is delivered. You can be firm without being cruel, honest without being harsh, and corrective without condemning.

1 Peter 3:8 calls us to be *"tenderhearted."*
That means correction should come from a place of care, not irritation.

A compassionate leader understands:

- Timing matters
- Tone matters
- Context matters
- Relationship matters

People receive corrections best when they know you genuinely care about them. Compassion ensures that truth wrapped in grace is not diluted but delivered in love.

Just about everyone I know has an elder in the family who can tell it like it is. They can confront the harsh reality of a situation head-on and put you in your place. They let you know how badly you messed up and make no mistake about it such behavior will not be tolerated!

They mince no words. Yet the entire time you're being chastised you have no doubt that it comes from a place of love. And when it's all said and done you walk away knowing that you're better because someone compassionately corrected your shortfall.

Compassion is a Witness

Compassion is one of the clearest reflections of Christ in the life of a leader. Jesus consistently showed compassion to the hurting, the overlooked, the broken, and the misunderstood. When leaders demonstrate compassion, they testify of His character without saying a word.

Maya Angelou once said, *"I've learned that people will forget what you said, people will forget what you did, but people will never forget how you made them feel."* Compassion is the leadership quality that shapes how people feel in your presence—safe, seen, valued, and understood.

Compassion draws people closer. It softens resistance. It builds bridges where walls once existed. It transforms environments filled with tension, fear, or discouragement into environments of hope, healing, and safety. People may forget your instructions, but they will never forget your compassion.

Practical Takeaways

1. Compassion is strength expressed through understanding, patience, and grace.

2. Daily actions — not dramatic gestures — reveal a leader's compassion.

3. Compassion communicates dignity and makes people feel valued.

4. Correction delivered with compassion strengthens relationships.

5. Compassion reflects the character of Christ and builds unity.

Reflection & Action Steps

1. Identify one person who needs your patience or understanding this week.

2. Reflect on moments when God showed compassion to you — how can you extend that to others?

3. Ask yourself: Do people feel safe approaching you with struggles or concerns?

4. Practice compassionate correction with someone who needs guidance.

5. Slow down once today to truly listen to someone without rushing or dismissing.

Closing Thoughts…

Compassion is not optional — it is essential. It is the ethical standard that humanizes leadership and reflects the heart of Christ. Compassion strengthens unity, deepens relationships, heals wounds, and creates safe spaces where people can grow.

When you practice compassion, you honor God, elevate others, and embody the kind of leadership that truly makes a difference. Compassion says to people, *"You matter to God, and you matter to me."* That message can transform lives. And transformed people are productive people.

Chapter 9

Fairness – The Measure of Faith-based Leadership

"Dishonest scales are an abomination to the Lord, But a just weight is His delight"

– Proverbs 11:1

Fairness is equality applied with empathy. As a leader, fairness means setting standards and sticking to them — whether dealing with clients, contracts, or colleagues. Favoritism fractures teams, but fairness fuels unity. It's not about making everyone happy; it's about making sure everyone is treated justly and equitably. Leaders who practice fairness don't play favorites — they play by principles.

Fairness – The Standard of Justice

Fairness is the ethical standard that keeps leadership upright, consistent, and honorable. It is the discipline of treating people with equity, impartiality, and integrity. It's not based on favoritism, emotion, personality, or personal preference. Fairness says, *"I will judge situations justly and honestly, treat people consistently, and make decisions that reflect justice rather than bias."*

"But the wisdom that is from above is first pure, then peaceable, gentle, willing to yield, full of mercy and good fruits, without partiality and without hypocrisy."

— James 3:17 NKJV

Leaders who operate with fairness create environments where people feel safe, valued, and respected. When fairness is present, trust increases. When fairness is absent, resentment grows. Fairness is the subtle influence that stabilizes teams, protects unity, and maintains credibility. It communicates to people: *"You will be treated with the same dignity, standard, and honesty as everyone else."*

Fairness Beyond Policy

Fairness is not just a policy — it is a posture. It begins in the heart before it shows up in decisions. It flows from a leader who genuinely desires to do what is right, not what is easy. Easier paths include favoritism, knee-jerk reactions, emotional decision-making, and treating people differently based on how much they irritate or inspire you.

Fairness comes from a heart that values justice because God Himself is just. Leaders who strive for fairness recognize that personal bias is real, and unless they intentionally guard their hearts, emotion can masquerade as discernment. Fair leaders slow down long enough to ensure they are listening completely, evaluating carefully, and deciding prayerfully.

When fairness becomes one of your core values, it influences how you evaluate performance, how you correct behavior, how you distribute opportunities, and how you handle conflict. It removes suspicion, neutralizes favoritism, and reinforces unity. Fairness is quiet, but it carries weight.

Pastor Dexter O. Rowland, Sr. of The New Piney Grove Missionary Baptist Church in Decatur, Georgia once said *"never set a precedent that you cannot maintain. The decision you make for one person is how everyone else will expect to be treated under similar circumstances. Therefore, pray earnestly before making your leadership decisions"*. That sage advice has paid leadership dividends that cannot be measured in dollars and cents.

Fairness Everyday

Fairness is revealed through consistent actions over time, not just in major decisions. It shows up when leaders:

- Gather all the facts before forming an opinion
- Treat every person with dignity
- Correct issues without favoritism
- Refuse to act out of irritation or impulse
- Give credit where credit is due
- Apply the same standards to everyone, including themselves

Fairness creates environments where justice and equity are normal, and partiality has no place. It eliminates the "in crowd" and "out crowd" that destroys morale. It ignores "clique-ish" influences, and ensures that effort is recognized, not overlooked; and wrongdoing is addressed, not ignored regardless of who's who.

Fairness does not mean treating everyone *identically*. It means treating everyone *appropriately* — according to truth, equity, and justice.

Fairness Communicates Honor

When leaders are fair, they communicate honor to everyone involved. Fairness says, *"I respect you enough to handle this truthfully, consistently, and justly."*
People feel honored when:

- Their voice is heard

- Their concerns matter

- Their contributions are recognized

- They are evaluated honestly

- They are corrected respectfully

Fairness protects people from being used, overlooked, or misjudged. It also protects leaders from being manipulated by emotion, persuasion, or pressure. Honorable leaders are fair leaders, and fair leaders are honorable leaders.

Correcting with Fairness

Fairness has the opportunity to shine the brightest in moments of correction. Anyone can be fair when everything is smooth. But when conflict arises, bias tries to take the wheel.

Fair leaders:

- Don't assume

- Don't take sides prematurely

- Don't let personal friendship cloud judgment

- Don't punish one person for another person's behavior

- Don't let emotions interpret facts

Fairness listens fully, evaluates carefully, and corrects consistently. James 3:17 teaches that God's wisdom is *"without partiality and without hypocrisy."* Fair correction is free from favoritism, and it frees people to receive discipline without resentment. Fairness ensures that truth, not temperament, governs the decision.

I remember a situation in my leadership where I violated this principle without realizing the damage it would cause. A team member who was also a close friend had dropped the ball on a major responsibility. If it had been anyone else, I would've addressed it quickly, clearly, and firmly. But because it was my friend, I softened the correction. I minimized the issue. I allowed excuses I wouldn't have accepted from anyone else.

At first, it felt like grace... but it wasn't. It was favoritism.

When the rest of the team found out how lightly I handled it, their reaction was painful but justified. They weren't angry about the mistake — they were angry about the inconsistency. They felt betrayed because I held them to a standard I refused to apply to someone in my personal circle. And in that moment, I realized something: unfair leadership breaks trust faster than any failure in performance.

That experience taught me a vital lesson: If correction isn't consistent, it isn't fair. And if it isn't fair, it cannot be respected.

It humbled me, but it also changed me. Since then, I've committed to letting truth, not friendship, convenience, or emotion, govern my decisions.

Fairness Is a Witness

Fairness is a powerful testimony in a world driven by bias, favoritism, and hidden agendas. When leaders demonstrate fairness, they model the justice of God. People may not always like a fair decision, but they will respect it. Fairness communicates credibility, dependability, and spiritual maturity.

It tells people that their leader will weigh situations justly, evaluate honestly, and operate with integrity even when no one is watching.

Fairness heals division, strengthens unity, and elevates morale. It turns the workplace, ministry, or team into a healthy environment where people can thrive.

People may forget what you said, but they will never forget how fair — or unfair — you were.

Practical Takeaways

1. Fairness is justice in daily leadership — impartial, consistent, and principled.
2. Bias must be confronted intentionally because it never disappears on its own.
3. Fairness strengthens trust, unity, and team morale.
4. Fair correction leads to repentance; biased correction leads to resentment.
5. Fairness reflects the justice and character of God.

Reflection & Action Steps

1. Identify one area where your emotions tend to override fairness — and address it.
2. Reflect on a recent decision: Was it fair, or was it influenced by frustration, bias, or pressure?
3. Ask a trusted person if your leadership feels fair and consistent to them.
4. Commit to gathering all the facts before forming conclusions.
5. Practice fairness this week by recognizing someone's effort, listening fully, or correcting impartially.

Closing Thoughts...

Fairness is the ethical standard that keeps leaders grounded, trustworthy, and aligned with God's justice. It protects unity, strengthens relationships, and elevates credibility. Fairness says to people, *"I will treat you with dignity, consistency, and integrity."* And that kind of leadership earns respect, builds confidence, and honors Christ in every environment.

Chapter 10

Citizenship – The Duty of Faith-based Leadership

"For all the law is fulfilled in one word, even in this: 'You shall love your neighbor as yourself.'"

— Galatians 5:14 NKJV

Citizenship is the ethical standard that reminds leaders they are part of a community, not separate from it. It is the recognition that leadership is not simply about what you achieve personally, but how you contribute collectively.

Citizenship is the daily expression of *loving your neighbor as yourself.* It says, *"I am responsible for strengthening the people, the culture, and the environment where God has placed me."*

Leaders who embrace citizenship understand that their actions influence more than their personal reputation — they influence the unity, morale, and health of the entire organization. Citizenship is not measured by titles or talents, but by participation, contribution, and character. When citizenship is strong, the community thrives. When it is absent, the organization fragments.

Citizenship Begins with Identity

Citizenship begins with identity — knowing that you are part of a body, a team, a fellowship, or a mission bigger than yourself. Before it becomes an outward action, it is an inward conviction: *"I belong here, and I am responsible for what happens here."*

It requires humility. The kind of humility that recognizes everyone plays a vital part. Citizenship rejects the mindset of entitlement and embraces the mindset of service. It refuses to say, *"That's not my problem,"* and replaces it with, *"This community matters, so I'll do my part."*

When citizenship becomes one of your core values, it shapes:

- How you show up
- How you serve
- How you speak
- How you solve problems
- How you support others

It becomes obvious who is committed to the community and who is not. Citizenship doesn't draw attention to itself, yet it continually works for the betterment of the collective.

Citizenship Everyday

Citizenship is not demonstrated through grand speeches or dramatic moments. It shows up in the simple disciplines that strengthens the collective. Leaders demonstrate citizenship when they:

• Contribute to solutions rather than complain about problems

• Carry their share of the workload without needing to be chased or reminded

• Support organizational decisions publicly, even when they offered different opinions privately

• Honor processes, systems, and structures that keep the community healthy

• Take initiative to improve the environment instead of waiting for someone else to act

Citizenship is not glamorous, but it is foundational. A community cannot flourish on talent alone — it flourishes when the people within it act responsibly, respectfully, and lovingly toward one another. Citizenship is love in action.

Citizenship Communicates Commitment

Citizenship tells others, *"You can count on me."* It communicates reliability, maturity, and loyalty to the shared mission. People can feel strong citizenship when they see someone:

- Supporting the mission publicly and privately
- Speaking well of the organization
- Encouraging others
- Contributing ideas, effort, and energy
- Protecting the reputation of the community
- Choosing unity over personal preference

Citizenship is more than behavior — it is a declaration of commitment. It is refusing to be a consumer and choosing instead to be a contributor.

Citizenship's Witness

Galatians 5:14 calls believers to *"love your neighbor as yourself,"* and citizenship is one of the clearest demonstrations of that love. When leaders act with kindness, unity, consistency, and service, their behavior becomes a witness that points people to Christ.

People may disagree with your theology, but they cannot deny your integrity. They may debate your doctrine, but they cannot argue with your character. They may question your mission, but they will respect your citizenship.

Citizenship turns your leadership into a testimony. It lets your light shine before men — not through words, but through lifestyle.

Citizenship Protects Culture

Every community has a culture — the atmosphere, attitudes, and expectations that shape how people feel and function. Citizenship protects that culture by ensuring everyone does their part.

Poor citizenship creates gaps, forces others to overcompensate, and erodes morale. Strong citizenship strengthens unity, stabilizes the environment, and builds pride in belonging.

A healthy culture is not the result of a single great leader — it is the result of many responsible citizens working together with love, respect, and shared purpose.

Citizenship is stewardship of the environment God trusted you with.

Citizenship Extends Beyond the Building

Citizenship begins inside the organization, but it must never end there. Every business, church, and ministry is planted in a larger community — a neighborhood, a city, a school district, a marketplace — and with that placement comes responsibility. No organization exists in isolation. We are part of a broader ecosystem, and our presence should make that ecosystem stronger, healthier, and more hopeful.

Great leaders remind their people that the mission does not stop at the front door. Citizenship pushes us beyond comfort zones and familiar faces so we can serve the world we are called to impact. A church that only blesses itself has misunderstood its purpose. A business that only profits from a community without contributing to it is practicing consumption, not citizenship. Leaders must consistently lift the eyes of the people and point them outward toward the greater good.

Citizenship looks like:

- Volunteering time and skills for the wellbeing of the neighborhood
- Supporting local schools, shelters, and community programs
- Providing resources or relief during crisis or disaster
- Partnering with other organizations for community uplift
- Showing up where people are hurting, overlooked, or underserved

When leaders model outward-facing compassion, the organization follows. When leaders help people see beyond their own building, they help them see beyond themselves.

Citizenship says, *"We are here to make this community better because God placed us here on purpose."* And when an organization embraces its responsibility to the larger community, it earns trust, builds credibility, and becomes a light that cannot be ignored. You become the city on a hill who cannot be hidden (Matthew 5:14-16 NKJV).

Practical Takeaways

1. Citizenship is the daily expression of loving your neighbor as yourself.
2. Healthy communities grow when individuals contribute, not consume.
3. Strong citizenship strengthens unity inside the organization.
4. True citizenship extends beyond the building into the surrounding community.
5. Citizenship reflects Christ by elevating the collective over the individual.

Reflection & Action Steps

1. Identify one way you can contribute more responsibly within your organization.
2. Evaluate whether your actions strengthen unity or create subtle division.
3. Ask a trusted person whether you show up as a contributor or a consumer.
4. Choose one way your organization can bless the surrounding community this month.
5. Pray for deeper awareness of the community God placed you in and how you can serve it.

Closing Thoughts…

Citizenship is more than good behavior inside an organization — it is a lifestyle of commitment, responsibility, and service that strengthens the collective and reflects the heart of Christ. It calls leaders to look beyond personal preference and organizational convenience and to invest in the greater good. Citizenship builds unity internally and impact externally.

When you practice citizenship, you are saying to God, *"I will steward the place You planted me,"* and to people, *"You can count on me to carry my part of the mission."*

This is the essence of Doing Small Better™ — contributing faithfully where you are, strengthening the community around you, and leaving every environment better than you found it.

CONCLUSION

Will You be Found Faithful?

"Moreover, it is required in stewards that one be found faithful."

— *1 Corinthians 4:2 NKJV*

Faithfulness Over a Few

If there's one truth that echoes through every chapter of this book, it's this: God honors faithfulness in the few.

Doing small better isn't just about leading efficiently — it's about leading *righteously.*
It's about choosing stewardship over ownership, compassion over competition, purpose over profit, and excellence over excuses.

In a world obsessed with scaling, God still celebrates *steady.* He still smiles on leaders who keep showing up, keep doing right, and keep trusting Him with the rest.

Because every small act of obedience becomes the seed of something significant.

You Were Chosen for This

You're not leading by accident. You've been *assigned* to your corner of influence — whether it's a business, a ministry, a team, or a community.

God didn't call you to be famous; He called you to be faithful. He didn't call you to impress the masses; He called you to impact the ones in front of you. When you embrace that, you'll stop comparing your platform to others and start cultivating the one God gave you. Because what seems small in your hands can still be supernatural in His.

Doing Small Better as a Way of Life

Doing small better isn't simply a slogan — it's a lifestyle.

It's how you build relationships, how you manage resources, and how you respond when things don't go your way. It's a mindset that says, *"I may not control the size of my stage, but I can control the way I deliver my lines."*

It's faith in action. It's integrity in motion. It's excellence on display.

Every conversation, every contract, every challenge is an opportunity to show the world what faith-based leadership looks like in real time and to show God that He chose a trustworthy steward.

Reminder to Prosper With Purpose

There's nothing wrong with wanting to prosper.
But remember this — *prosperity without purpose is hollow, and purpose without prosperity is incomplete.*

True prosperity is the harmony of both.

When your heart is aligned with God's will, and your hands are diligent in His work, profit becomes the byproduct of purpose.

That's the kind of prosperity that lets you rest at night, smile in storms, and give freely because you've already been blessed abundantly.

The Ripple Effect

Every business you build, every team you lead, every sermon you preach, every home you restore — it all ripples outward.

The people you serve today will carry your influence into their tomorrows.

The integrity you model will multiply in ways you'll never see.

Your obedience today becomes someone else's inspiration tomorrow.

That's the quiet power of faith-based leadership: it outlives you.

> *"The memory of the righteous is blessed."*
> — *Proverbs 10:7*

Your Turn

This is your moment. You've read the principles, reflected on the stories, and rediscovered the importance of doing small better. Now it's time to put it into practice.

Lead with conviction. Serve with compassion. Operate with excellence. Sleep with peace.
And trust that God — the ultimate Builder — will bless the work of your hands.

When you do small better, you're not just running a business —you're building a legacy.
You're not just managing people — you're ministering to hearts. You're not just chasing profits — you're fulfilling purpose.

And one day, when your race is finished and your work is done, may you hear the words that every faithful leader longs to hear:

> *"His lord said to him, 'Well done, good and faithful servant; you were faithful over a few things, I will make you ruler over many.'"*

> — *Matthew 25:23 NKJV*

Final Reflection & Prayer

Reflection:
What one principle from this book are you most determined to live out starting today?

Prayer:

Heavenly Father, thank You for entrusting me with purpose, people, and possibility. Teach me to lead with integrity, to serve with compassion, and to start and finish with faith. Help me to see small not as insignificant, but as sacred. May my life and leadership reflect Your character, my work honor Your name, and my legacy point others to You. In Jesus' name, Amen.

www.ingramcontent.com/pod-product-compliance
Lightning Source LLC
Chambersburg PA
CBHW060427090426
42734CB00011B/2475